DNA

Contents

DNA   2

How DNA Is Used to Prove a Person's Identity   8
Case Study: the Romanov Family   10

How DNA Is Used to Prove Paternity and Maternity   12
Case Study: Anna Anderson   14

How DNA Is Used in Genealogy   17
Case Study: the Maori People   18

How DNA Is Used in Forensic Science   20

How DNA Is Used in Genetic Medicine   24

DNA and the Future   26

By Lee-Ann Wright

DNA

Predict

What do you think DNA might be about?

Cells are the tiny building blocks that make up every living organism. Some organisms have only one cell, while other organisms, such as humans, have billions of cells. Humans have hundreds of different types of cells, which all have special functions (nerve, skin, muscle, bone) and these cells are continually being replaced by new cells as old cells die.

Found in almost every cell are strands of material called DNA – the blueprint that makes up the human body, and the instructions that make the body work. DNA is made up of two long strands that lock together, which makes it look like a long, twisted ladder. This shape is called a double helix. As the human body grows, DNA can copy itself by splitting into two halves, so that any new cells produced contain exact copies of that same DNA.

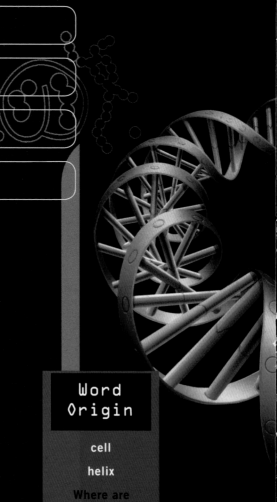

Word Origin

cell

helix

Where are they from?

Clarify

nucleus

blueprint

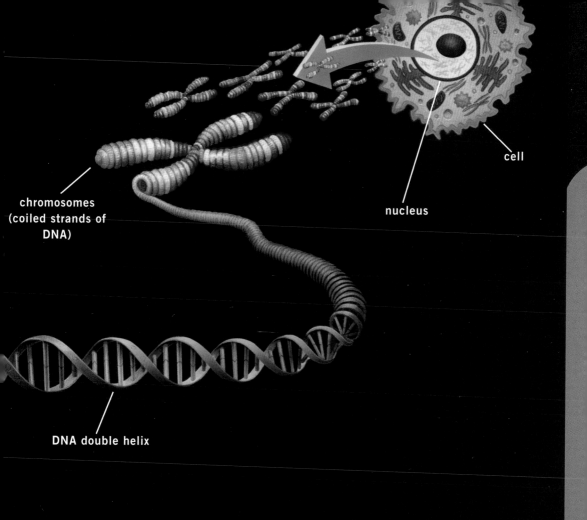

cell

nucleus

chromosomes
(coiled strands of
DNA)

DNA double helix

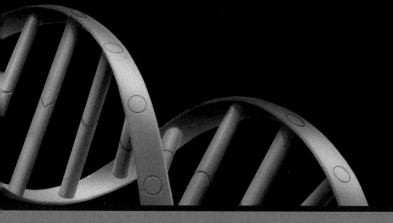

DNA is broken up into smaller segments called genes. Each person has thousands of genes, which they pass on to their children, and which they inherited from their mother and father, who inherited them from *their* mother and father, and so on. Genes are what determine a person's characteristics, such as how they look – hair, skin, eye colour and height – some of their behaviour, and even if they will inherit certain diseases or conditions.

Family members have similar characteristics because of the genes passed from generation to generation.

DNA in genes is what makes each person unique, and no two people have the same DNA except for identical twins.

The DNA in genes is made up of a chemical code, represented by the letters A, T, G and C. Each gene has the same letters, but written in a different code. Scientists call this code the "genetic code".

Clarify

characteristics

unique

Genetic Code

DNA is written in a long code of four letters, A, T, G and C.	ATGCTCGAATAAATGTGAATTTGA
The letters are divided into "words".	ATG CTC GAA TAA ATG TGA ATT TGA
The words make sentences. Geneticists call these "sentences" genes.	ATG CTC GAA TAA ATG TGA ATT TGA

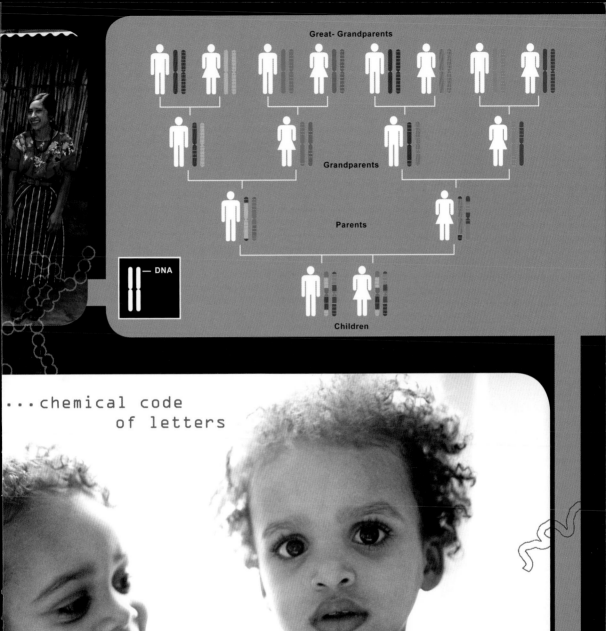

Great- Grandparents

Grandparents

— DNA

Parents

Children

...chemical code
of letters

Question

How do you think it is
possible for twins to
have the same DNA?

Identical twins share the same DNA, but not the same fingerprints.

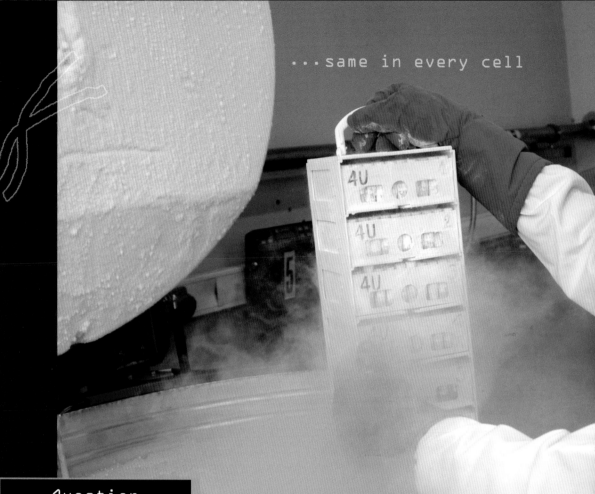

Question

Why do you think geneticists would want to study the evolution of human populations?

This geneticist is using liquid nitrogen to store cells that will be used to study genetic disorders.

Clarify

evolution

inherited disorder

Forensic investigators search a crime scene for DNA.

DNA sequences are compared to prove maternity or paternity.

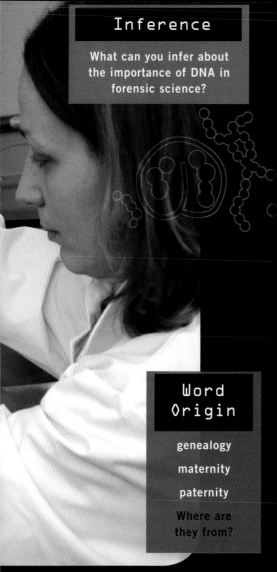

Inference

What can you infer about the importance of DNA in forensic science?

Scientists who study genes and the genetic code are called geneticists. Geneticists do not yet know the function of every human gene, but they do understand much about the genetic code carried in the DNA of a human body.

A person has a DNA profile that is different from anybody else's, just like their fingerprints. A DNA profile is the same in every cell of a person and cannot be changed.

Geneticists study and analyse these DNA profiles for many different reasons, including:

- proving a person's identity,
- maternity and paternity testing,
- tracing the evolution of human populations (genealogy),
- forensic science,
- studying genetic medicine and inherited disorders.

Word Origin

genealogy

maternity

paternity

Where are they from?

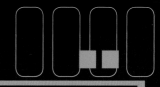

Key Points

- Scientists who study genes and the genetic code are called geneticists.

?

Interesting Facts

?

Visual Challenge

In what other ways could you present this information?

How DNA Is Used to Prove a Person's Identity

Every day, all over the world, thousands of people go missing or die for many different reasons, including accidents and natural disasters.

Geneticists can determine someone's identity by analysing their DNA, which can be extracted from hair, bone or human tissue. The DNA is then compared to DNA from the families of missing people to see if a match can be made.

TA-0664

TA-0654

Inference

What can you infer about the DNA of family members?

Clarify

identity

extracted

These tags at a burial site of tsunami victims have numbers that refer to DNA records.

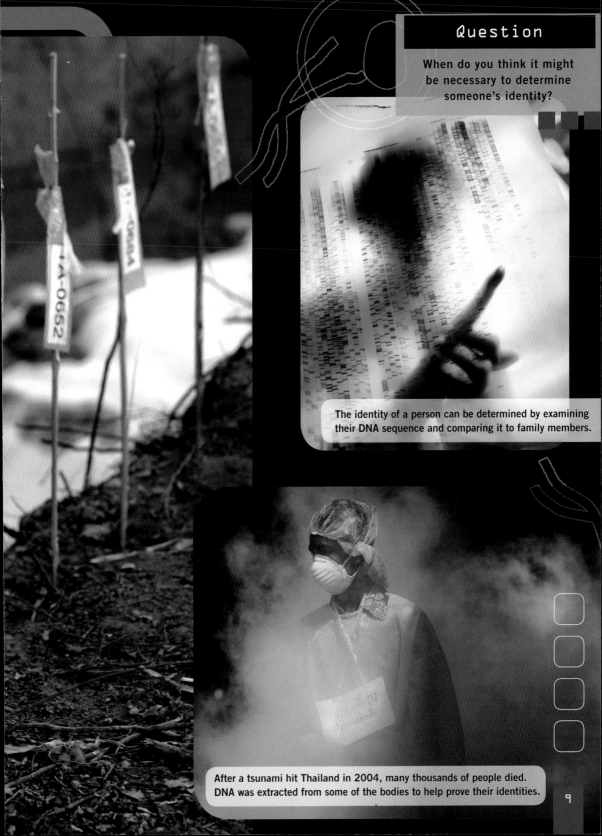

Question

When do you think it might be necessary to determine someone's identity?

The identity of a person can be determined by examining their DNA sequence and comparing it to family members.

After a tsunami hit Thailand in 2004, many thousands of people died. DNA was extracted from some of the bodies to help prove their identities.

9

Case Study: The Romanov Family

In 1918, the last Russian emperor, Tsar Nicholas II, his wife Tsarina Alexandra and their entire family were shot and killed by soldiers. The family doctor, a nurse and two servants were also killed. They were then buried in a grave in Siberia, which was kept secret for more than 73 years.

In 1991, scientists uncovered what they thought might be the grave containing the Romanov family. Any bodies in the grave would have been buried for a long time, in sometimes very severe weather conditions, and the scientists were sceptical about being able to retrieve any DNA from the skeletal remains.

The skeletons of nine people were discovered, which puzzled the scientists, as eleven people had reportedly been killed. The skeletons were taken away and tested for DNA, which was discovered in the bones and skulls.

The family tree of Tsarina Alexandra showed there was a maternal relative still alive in England.

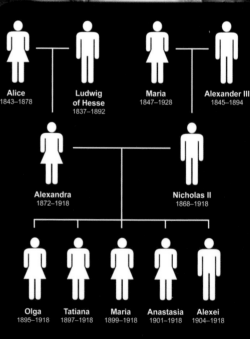

| Alice 1843–1878 | Ludwig of Hesse 1837–1892 | Maria 1847–1928 | Alexander III 1845–1894 |

| Alexandra 1872–1918 | Nicholas II 1868–1918 |

| Olga 1895–1918 | Tatiana 1897–1918 | Maria 1899–1918 | Anastasia 1901–1918 | Alexei 1904–1918 |

Romanov family tree

Clarify

severe

sceptical

... scientists
were sceptical

Tsar Nicholas and Tsarina Alexandra with their children (from left to right) Olga, Maria, Anastasia, Alexei and Tatiana.

Scientists obtained a sample of DNA from the relative, Prince Philip of England, which matched the DNA in four of the skeletons. Scientists were then able to prove they were the skeletons of Alexandra and her daughters Olga, Tatiana and Maria.

According to the family tree of Tsar Nicholas, James, Duke of Fife was a maternal relative of his. He gave his DNA for comparison, allowing scientists to prove that one of the skeletons was Tsar Nicholas II.

Scientists concluded the skeletons of Prince Alexei and Princess Anastasia were both missing from the grave. The four other skeletons were most likely the doctor, the nurse and the two servants, as their DNA did not match any of the other skeletons.

Question Generate

What questions could you ask about this information?

How DNA Is Used to Prove Paternity and Maternity

Geneticists can determine a person's paternity, maternity, or even both, by analysing their DNA.

Segments of DNA, or genes, are passed down from parents to their children through inheritance. This means that no child has DNA that neither of their parents has, and DNA from close relatives will be more similar than DNA from unrelated people.

DNA is often used to prove paternity or maternity in cases of adoption or mistaken identity. Many missing children have been reunited with their parents after spending years apart.

In 2004, DNA tests proved that Delimar Vera (right) was the missing daughter of Luz Aida Cuevas (left).

...reunited with their parents

Key Points

- Geneticists can determine a person's paternity, maternity, or even both, by analysing their DNA.

?

Interesting Facts

?

Clarify

inheritance

Visual Challenge

In what other ways could you present this information?

M   C   C   F

Question

Why do you think DNA
testing is used in cases
of adoption?

comparisons of DNA sequences of a family proving relationship between children and parents

Anastasia Romanov

Case Study: Anna Anderson

In 1921, a woman was pulled from a canal in Berlin, Germany, and committed to a psychiatric hospital. After refusing to reveal her identity for 18 months, she finally declared herself to be Princess Anastasia Romanov.

Since the execution of the Romanov family in 1918, many rumours had surfaced that some of the children may have survived, particularly Princess Anastasia.

After being released from the psychiatric hospital, the woman adopted the name of Anna Anderson and went to court to try to prove her royal identity. DNA testing had not yet been discovered, but all the other evidence was carefully examined. Anna had the same hair and eye colour, height and distinctive body markings as the princess. Anna even had a misshapen foot, just like the princess had. But she could not speak or read Russian, English or French like the Tsar's daughters.

The royal family did some of their own investigative work, and came to believe that she was Franziska Schanzkowska, who had gone missing from a Berlin boarding house.

Word Origin

committed

psychiatric

Where are they from?

a young Anna Anderson

After two decades, the German court found that Anna Anderson could not prove that she was Princess Anastasia. Anna moved to the US, married and lived out her days in Virginia. She died in 1984 without the world knowing her true identity.

The mystery of Anna Anderson was not solved until a preserved piece of her intestine from an operation she had undergone in 1979 was discovered at a hospital.

In 1994, Anna's DNA was tested and compared to DNA discovered in the skeletal remains of the Romanov family. It proved that Anna had no paternal or maternal link to the Romanov family. She was not the daughter of Tsar Nicholas II or Tsarina Alexandra, nor was she a relative of any of the royal family.

Scientists compared Anna's DNA samples with DNA provided by Schanzkowska's great nephew Karl Maucher. The DNA matched, proving that she was paternally and maternally linked to the Schanzkowska family. Anna Anderson was in fact Franziska Schanzkowska.

The ears of Anastasia (top) and Anna (bottom) were compared in the trial.

Opinion

What is your opinion of DNA testing to determine someone's identity?

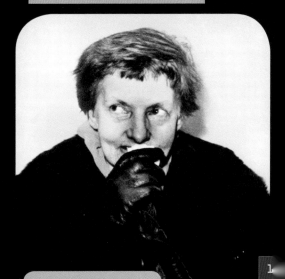

Anna Anderson later in life

...the DNA matched

Clarify

preserved

investigative

Scientists study DNA to trace the genetic links between certain groups of people.

Question

Why do you think geneticists study and trace the genealogy of different ethnic groups?

How DNA Is Used in Genealogy

African-Americans can use DNA to trace their African heritage.

Because DNA contains information that can be passed down from generation to generation with little change, it can be used to study and trace the genealogies of different families. It can also be used to help find out where different ethnic groups originally came from, how they migrated and how they have changed over thousands of years.

Geneticists have been able to trace human genetic links as far back as 60,000 years. They have also traced different ethnic groups who share common DNA all over the world.

Scientists have traced the gene for ginger hair back thousands of years through DNA.

Clarify

generation

ethnic

17

Case Study: The Maori People

Through DNA, a genealogical link has been made between the Maori people of New Zealand and the Polynesian people of the Cook Islands. Polynesians from the Cook Islands set off on journeys to find uninhabited islands, which led to the discovery of New Zealand about 1000 years ago.

Geneticists also believe that the closest genetic relatives to the Maori and Polynesian people are found in Taiwan. DNA links between Maori and the native people of Taiwan go back as far as 5000 years. Apart from their DNA, they have similar traditional cultures, speak similar languages and there are similarities in their appearance.

Maori New Zealander Nathan Rarere traced his ancestry to Taiwan through DNA analysis. He is pictured with a woman from the native Taiwanese Narawan people.

...DNA links go back 5000 years

Inference

... the closest genetic relatives to Maori and Polynesian people are found in Taiwan.

What can you infer from this?

Maori woman with a traditional tattoo

Narawan woman wearing traditional dress

Maori woman wearing traditional dress

Narawan woman with a traditional tattoo

19

How DNA Is Used in Forensic Science

Inference

DNA evidence is more sensitive than other types of evidence.

What can you infer from this text?

Any person involved in a crime usually leaves behind some tiny clue or evidence at the crime scene. This evidence is broken into two types, physical evidence and biological evidence. Biological evidence contains DNA and is not always visible to the naked eye. It can be found anywhere at the crime scene, in the form of skin, hair, saliva and other human tissue. It can be used to identify the victim and the perpetrator. It can also be used to identify witnesses, possible suspects and accomplices.

DNA evidence is more sensitive than other types of evidence. Forensic investigators wear special clothing and use extreme caution at a crime scene.

Forensic investigators can retrieve and analyse DNA found at a crime scene. They check it to see if it matches the DNA of a suspect. A computer system called CODIS (combined DNA index system) can also be used. CODIS contains the DNA profiles of convicted offenders.

Forensic investigators can compare DNA profiles found at the crime scene to ones in CODIS. If the DNA matches exactly, the suspect is more than likely guilty. If the DNA does not match, the tests can prove the suspect's innocence.

Clarify

biological evidence

physical evidence

accomplices

perpetrator

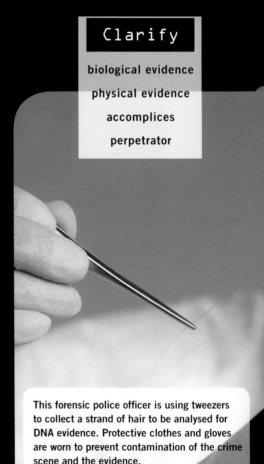

This forensic police officer is using tweezers to collect a strand of hair to be analysed for DNA evidence. Protective clothes and gloves are worn to prevent contamination of the crime scene and the evidence.

Why do you think forensic investigators use extreme caution at a crime scene?

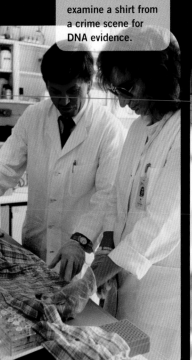

Forensic scientists examine a shirt from a crime scene for DNA evidence.

a police forensic team examining a crime scene

...the tests can prove the suspect's innocence

Key Points

- Biological evidence contains DNA.

?

Interesting Facts

?

Visual Challenge

In what other ways could you present this information?

Larry Peterson walks out of jail after 17 years behind bars. DNA analysis cast doubt on his conviction.

...hundreds of people have now been freed

Opinion

Do you think DNA should be used for every case? Why or why not?

DNA evidence can prove the innocence or guilt of a person. Before DNA testing was discovered, many people were convicted for crimes they did not commit, and some guilty people were thought to be innocent.

With the help of DNA, hundreds of people have now been freed from prisons after serving time for crimes they did not commit. DNA has also helped solve hundreds of "cold cases".

Clarify
the Term

cold case

DNA proved the innocence of Luis Diaz, freed from jail after serving 26 years for a crime he did not commit.

How DNA Is Used in Genetic Medicine

Geneticists can analyse people's DNA to determine whether their DNA genetic code has any "spelling mistakes" in it.

Mistakes in DNA may include a repeated piece of DNA, a missing piece of DNA or a change in the DNA code. These mistakes are called mutations and can cause different conditions in people. Geneticists have worked out that about 3000 diseases are passed down from generation to generation through inheritance.

Geneticists can study the DNA of a person who has a particular disease and compare their DNA to relatives with the same disease. The DNA can then be compared with healthy families, which allows the geneticists to find the inherited gene that causes the disease.

Geneticists now know so much about the human genetic code, they can actually alter it in a process called genetic engineering.

Clarify

mutations

...3000 diseases are passed
down from generation to generation

This magnified picture shows cell material being injected into a cell for cancer research.

DNA and the Future

Since the discovery of DNA in 1953, geneticists have learned much about the structure, role and importance of DNA in human beings and other organisms.

The human genome project, which started in 1988 and was completed in 2003, allowed geneticists to map out the entire genetic code of human DNA. But making a map of human DNA is not the same as understanding what DNA does. Geneticists have yet to work out what thousands of different genes do and how they do it.

There have also been many advances in the technology of genetic engineering. It is used in agriculture, food, medicine, animals and human beings.

People have many different opinions about genetic engineering. Some argue that it is a safe technology and the way forward for the future. Others argue that it is dangerous and could have unforseen consequences, and that geneticists should not be tampering with nature.

Dolly the sheep was the first animal to be cloned by scientists.

Key Points

- The human genome project allowed geneticists to map out the entire genetic code of human DNA.

?

Interesting Facts

?

Visual Challenge

In what other ways could you present this information?

A scientist takes a DNA sample from a banana plant for cloning.

Index

cells 2

DNA profiles 7, 20

double helix................................2

forensic science 7, 20
 CODIS 20
 cold cases............................23
 forensic investigators 20
 proving innocence 20, 23

genealogy 7, 17
 Maori...................................18
 native Taiwanese 18

genes......................... 4, 7, 12, 26

genetic code 4, 7, 24, 26

genetic engineering................24, 27

genetic medicine 7, 24

geneticists..............7, 8, 12, 17, 18,
 24, 26-27

human genome project..................26

identical twins 4

inherited diseases
 /conditions......................4, 7, 24

maternity and paternity.............7, 12
 Anna Anderson.................. 14-15

proving identity 7, 8
 missing children....................12
 natural disasters.....................8

Romanov family........... 10-11, 14-15

Think about the Text

Making connections – what connections can you make to the information presented in *DNA*?

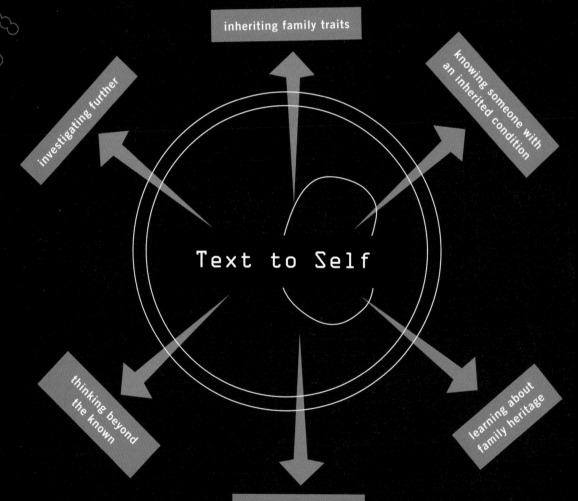

inheriting family traits

knowing someone with an inherited condition

investigating further

Text to Self

learning about family heritage

thinking beyond the known

using knowledge to help people

Text to Text

Talk about other informational texts you may have read that have similar features. Compare the texts.

Text to World

Talk about situations in the world that might connect to elements in the text.

Planning an Informational Explanation

1 Select a topic that explains why something is the way it is or how something works.

2 Make a mind map of questions about the topic.

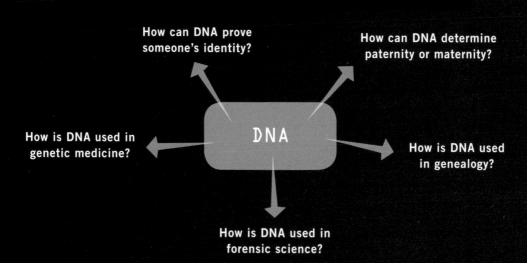

How can DNA prove someone's identity?

How can DNA determine paternity or maternity?

How is DNA used in genetic medicine?

DNA

How is DNA used in genealogy?

How is DNA used in forensic science?

3 Locate the information you will need.

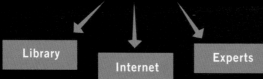

Library

Internet

Experts

4 Organise your information using the questions you selected as headings.

5 Make a plan.

Introduction:

> Found in almost every cell are strands of material called DNA – the blueprint that makes up the human body.

Points in a coherent and logical sequence:

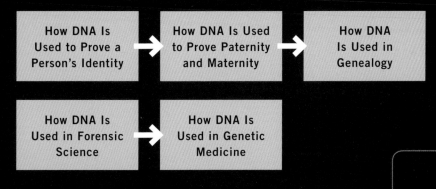

| How DNA Is Used to Prove a Person's Identity | → | How DNA Is Used to Prove Paternity and Maternity | → | How DNA Is Used in Genealogy |

| How DNA Is Used in Forensic Science | → | How DNA Is Used in Genetic Medicine |

6 Design some visuals to include in your explanation. You can use graphs, diagrams, labels, charts, tables, cross-sections...

Writing an Informational Explanation

Have you...

- explored causes and effects?

- used scientific and technical vocabulary?

- used the present tense? (Most explanations are written in the present tense.)

- written in a formal style that is concise and accurate?

- avoided unnecessary descriptive details, metaphors or similes?

- avoided author bias or opinion?

Don't forget to revisit your writing. Do you need to change, add or delete anything to improve your explanation?